Rookie
Read-About® Science

Solids, Liquids, and Gases

By Ginger Garrett

Consultant
Linda Bullock
Science Curriculum Specialist

Children's Press®
A Division of Scholastic Inc.
New York   Toronto   London   Auckland   Sydney
Mexico City   New Delhi   Hong Kong
Danbury, Connecticut

Designer: Herman Adler Design
Photo Researcher: Caroline Anderson
The photo on the cover shows a cold glass of water illustrating the concept
of solids (ice), liquids (water), and gases (condensation).

Library of Congress Cataloging-in-Publication Data

Garrett, Ginger, 1968–
  Solids, liquids, and gases / by Ginger Garrett ; consultant Linda Bullock.
    p. cm.— (Rookie read-about science)
  Includes index.
  ISBN 0-516-23615-6 (lib. bdg.)   0-516-24663-1 (pbk.)
  1. Matter—Properties—Juvenile literature. I. Title. II. Series.
  QC173.36.G38 2004
  530.4—dc22

                                    2004001219

14 15 R 13   62

What is made of matter?

Everything you hear and see is made of matter. So is everything you feel, touch, and taste.

Matter can be a solid, liquid, or gas. All matter takes up space.

Solid matter has a shape.
It takes up space. Ice is
solid matter.

You can see it, feel it,
touch it, and taste it. You
can hear it when it cracks.

Ice is frozen water.
When ice melts, it turns
into a liquid.

Liquid water is matter.
It takes up space just like
ice. But it does not keep
the same shape.

Pour some liquid water into a glass. What happens?

The water takes the same shape as the glass. Ice does not do that.

Watch what happens to liquid water in a teakettle. In time, the water boils inside the kettle.

What comes out of the spout?

Steam comes out. Steam is water, too.

Steam is not a solid or liquid. It is a gas.

A gas is matter. You cannot always see a gas. But you can often smell it, taste it, or feel it.

Watch a lighted candle.
A candle is solid matter.

The candle melts. It turns
from solid matter to liquid
matter.

Now, blow out the light. What do you see?

Smoke rises in the air. The smoke is a gas. You can smell it. It spreads through the air.

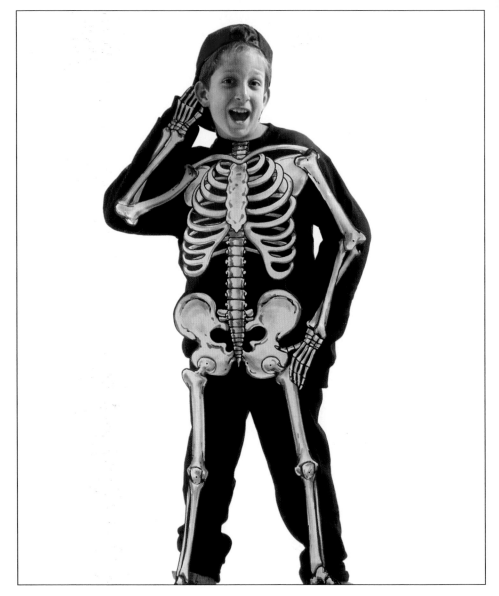

You are made of matter.
There are solids, liquids,
and gases inside your body.

Can you name something
solid in your body?

Bones!

Your bones are solid matter.
Bones take up space. They
keep their shape.

Your bones help you hop,
skip, jump, and run.

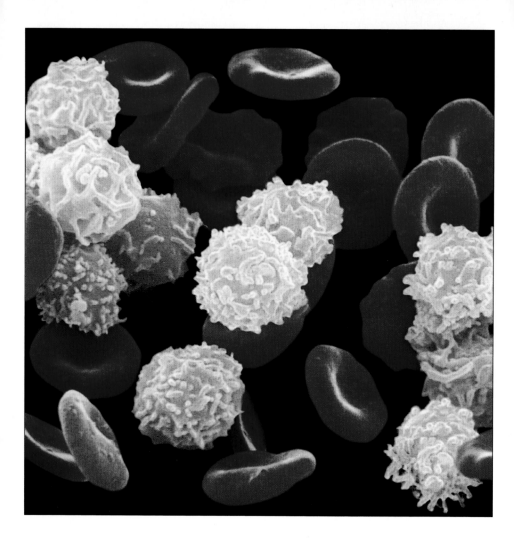

Your blood is liquid matter.

Blood flows into every part of your body. It fills your fingers. It fills your toes. You are full of liquid matter.

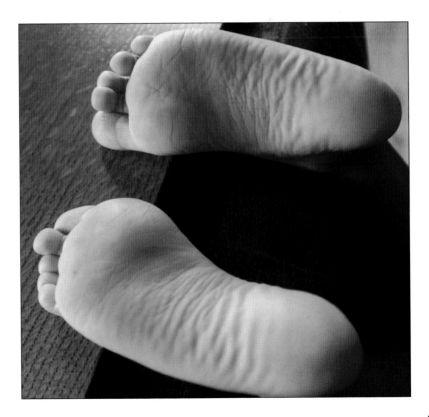

Your lungs are filled
with air. Air is a gas.

You breathe gas in.
You breathe gas out.
Your lungs are filled
with gas matter.

You are made of matter.
So is everything you can
see and hear and touch.

The whole world is made
of solids, liquids, and gases.

Words You Know

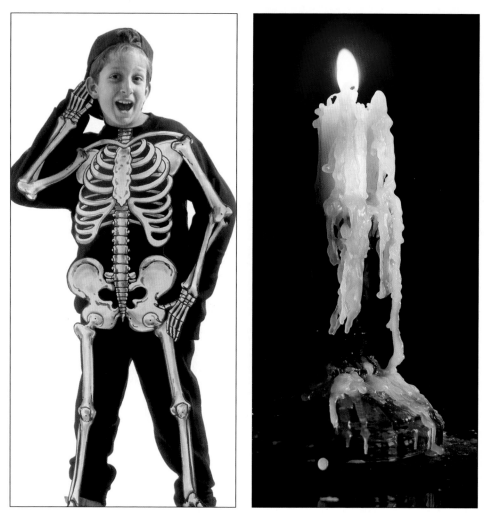

bones   candle

ice

steam

water

Index

About the Author

Ginger Garrett is a writer who lives in Georgia. She is made of solids, liquids, and gases. She has written for inventors and doctors and bankers who are also made up of solids, liquids, and gases.

Photo Credits

Photographs © 2004: Ellen B. Senisi: cover, 16, 19, 25, 30 right; Peter Arnold Inc./Norbert Wu: 7; PhotoEdit: 11, 31 bottom (Bill Aron), 12, 31 top right (Deborah Davis), 4, 20, 30 left (Richard Hutchings), 26 (David Young Wolff); The Image Works: 3 (Bill Bachmann), 8, 31 top left (Eastcott-Momatiuk), 15 (Kent Meireis), 29 (Sjkold), 23 (Mitch Wojnarowicz); Visuals Unlimited/David M. Phillips: 24.